D0772210

WITHDRAWN

JOPLIN TORNADO
SURVIVAL STORIES

BY EMILY O'KEEFE

Published by The Child's World®
1980 Lookout Drive • Mankato, MN 56003-1705
800-599-READ • www.childsworld.com

Acknowledgments
The Child's World®: Mary Berendes, Publishing Director
Red Line Editorial: Design, editorial direction, and production
Photographs ©: Mike Gullett/AP Images, cover, 1, 17; Ed Zurga/Reuters/Corbis, 6;
Mark Schiefelbein/AP Images, 9; Charlie Riedel/AP Images, 10; iStockphoto, 12,
21; Mike Theiss/National Geographic/Getty Images, 14; Shane Bevel/ABC/Getty
Images, 18; Paul Sancya/AP Images, 22; Steve Froebe/iStockphoto, 25; Pablo Martinez
Monsivais/AP Images, 27; Melissa Brandes/Shutterstock Images, 28

ISBN 9781634074261

LCCN 2015946318

Printed in the United States of America
Mankato, MN
December, 2015
PA02288

ABOUT THE AUTHOR

Emily O'Keefe has worked as an author, editor, and teacher. She often writes
books and articles for young people. O'Keefe holds a PhD in English from
Loyola University. She lives in Chicago, Illinois.

TABLE OF
CONTENTS

DISASTER STRIKES

At 5:11 p.m. on May 22, 2011, an emergency siren blared in Joplin, Missouri. The siren warned that severe weather was coming. Most residents ignored the alert. The sky was sunny and clear. Few realized that a devastating tornado was on its way.

As the storm approached, radio and television stations announced tornado warnings. A second emergency siren sounded at 5:38 p.m. Many people prepared for the storm. But the storm came quickly, and some people were too slow to take **refuge**. By 5:41 p.m., the tornado had reached the edges of Joplin. Soon, it was roaring through the city.

By 6:12 p.m., the storm had ended. In a short time, it had done an incredible amount of damage. The tornado destroyed nearly 7,000 houses. It killed 161 people, making it the seventh-deadliest tornado in U.S. history. It was also one of the largest. The path of the tornado was 6 miles (9.7 km) long. It was nearly 1 mile (1.6 km) wide.

Though many people died in the storm, others had dramatic tales of survival. After the storm, they worked to locate missing people and help one another recover from injuries. Today, survivors are continuing to rebuild their community in Joplin.

THE JOPLIN TORNADO, MAY 22, 2011

5:11 p.m.: The first emergency siren sounds.

5:17 p.m.: Radio and television stations announce a tornado warning.

5:34 p.m.: A severe thunderstorm becomes a tornado to the south of Joplin.

5:38 p.m.: The second emergency siren sounds.

5:41 p.m.: The tornado reaches southwest Joplin.

5:42 p.m.: Saint John's Regional Medical Center is hit by the tornado.

5:49 p.m.: The tornado hits nearly every building on Main Street.

5:54 p.m.: The tornado grows to one mile (1.6 km) wide.

5:57 p.m.: Atmosphere changes begin to weaken the tornado.

6:12 p.m.: The tornado ends.

Chapter 1

TORNADO IN THE EMERGENCY ROOM

May 22, 2011, was a quiet afternoon at Saint John's Regional Medical Center in Joplin. Nurses and doctors checked on patients. Guests visited sick family members. Some were eating meals or watching television.

Nurse Angie Abner was helping patients in the emergency room. She had worked at Saint John's for about a year. Before that, she had worked as a firefighter and **paramedic**. She was used to helping people during emergencies.

In the early evening, Abner's coworker announced that a tornado was possible. Abner and the other nurses started to move equipment out of the hallways. That way, they could help patients get to a safer area if the storm hit. Still, few people at the hospital thought they were in real danger. "Of course, no one ever thinks it's going to happen," Abner said later.[1] After ten minutes,

◄ **A tree stripped of its leaves and bark stands outside Saint John's Regional Medical Center on May 23, 2011.**

the sky turned green. A green sky is a sign that a tornado might be coming.

A security guard ran toward the emergency room. "Take cover!" he yelled. "We're gonna get hit!"[2] Abner and other hospital staff scrambled to help patients take shelter. Soon afterward, the glass windows in the emergency room shattered. Doors flew open and machines fell over. "Everything just started flying at me," Abner recalled.[3] While the winds whipped through the building, she crawled down the hallway to check on patients.

Minutes later, the tornado had passed. But Abner's job had just begun. There were 183 patients in the hospital. Many were too ill or injured to move. Some were trapped under **debris** from the tornado. Doctors and nurses ran to check on people and treat their injuries. Abner knew she had to keep working for the sake of those who could not help themselves.

By this time, the hospital was dark. The storm had caused the power to go out and had destroyed the hospital's backup **generators**. Abner and the hospital staff gathered emergency supplies. Other nurses and doctors set up outdoor tents where they could treat patients. One doctor performed surgery using only a flashlight as a light source. Ambulance drivers took the patients with the worst injuries to other hospitals.

▲ A destroyed helicopter lies on its side near Saint John's Regional Medical Center after the storm.

Other injured tornado survivors began to arrive at the hospital. One woman, Lacey Eagleshield, had been hit in the head by tornado debris. She ran to the Saint John's emergency room, where Abner wrapped a cloth around her wound.

▲ Staff at Saint John's Regional Medical Center treated patients out of tents after the tornado destroyed much of the hospital building.

"She immediately stuck to me, put the towel to my head," Eagleshield said.[4]

Abner and the other nurses kept working to help the people of Joplin. Many survived thanks to their efforts. Eagleshield was one of the survivors. A few months after the storm, Abner moved to New Mexico to start a new job. But Eagleshield never forgot the nurse who helped her. In September 2011, Eagleshield appeared on a news program to give a special message to Abner. "I know how hard it must have been," she said. "Thank you for being so strong."[5]

FAST FACTS

Number of people who lived in Joplin at the time of the tornado	**50,175**
Number of people affected by the tornado	**17,000**
Number of people injured in the tornado	**1,150**
Number of people **displaced** by the tornado	**9,200**

Chapter 2

TAKING SHELTER AT A RESTAURANT

At 5:00 p.m. on May 22, 2011, an International House of Pancakes (IHOP) in Joplin was busy. Restaurant customers were celebrating school graduations and other events. Two local politicians were sharing meals with their families. Danny Khatib, the restaurant manager, was on duty. Another five workers and 30 customers were in the building.

Soon, the tornado sirens began to sound. People began talking about reports of a storm nearby. At first, Khatib was not concerned. Light rain began to fall, and clouds gathered in the sky. Since Joplin is in **Tornado Alley**, severe weather is common in the city. Many residents were used to sirens and storm warnings. But as the storm got worse, Khatib started to worry. Customers noticed that large hail was falling from the sky. One person spotted flying debris. Then, the power went out.

◄ **Danny Khatib and more than 30 others took refuge in Joplin's International House of Pancakes.**

The people in the restaurant did not have much time to react. The building started to shake. The ceiling began to cave in. Some people hid under tables. But Khatib knew of a safer place. The IHOP kept food in a big walk-in refrigerator and walk-in freezer in the back of the restaurant. Khatib knew these could protect people from flying furniture and other debris.

Khatib led customers to the back of the restaurant, where 15 people fit into the walk-in refrigerator. Another 15 people got into the walk-in freezer. A few others huddled in corners of the kitchen. For five minutes, they stayed and listened to the winds. The refrigerator and freezer were crowded and completely dark. But they provided shelter from the tornado. Khatib thought the wind sounded like a train. "You could hear the noises," he said. "Everybody got scared."[6]

Eventually, the winds became quieter. Khatib and the other IHOP workers got out to see if the storm had passed. The tornado had moved on. It had left the restaurant completely changed. Some parts were destroyed, but there was still food on some of the plates. Broken glass was everywhere. The walls of the building were gone. Later, Khatib learned that the storm had also demolished his home. But the freezer and refrigerator had kept

◀ **Lightning strikes near Joplin before the tornado sweeps through the town.**

JOPLIN BUSINESSES ONE YEAR LATER

The Joplin tornado destroyed hundreds of businesses. Some owners decided to close their damaged stores or restaurants for good. But by May 2012, one year after the tornado, many of the destroyed businesses had reopened.

553
businesses damaged
or destroyed by
the tornado

446
businesses that
reopened or were
planning to reopen

33
businesses that
decided not to rebuild

21
new businesses that
opened in Joplin

the people at the IHOP safe. Everyone in the restaurant survived the storm.

After the tornado hit the IHOP, Khatib vowed that it would "come back better than before."[9] Fifteen months after the disaster, the restaurant reopened.

A Joplin resident looks over the rubble of his home. Experts ▶ estimate the storm destroyed one-third of the city.

Chapter 3

SAVED BY A BICYCLE HELMET

Augie Ward was a student at Kelsey Norman Elementary School in Joplin. In October 2010, a speaker named Kevin Theilen came to talk to Augie's class about bicycle safety. Theilen was a firefighter and a leader of Missouri's Safe Kids program. He gave each student in Augie's class a free bicycle helmet. Theilen knew that safety gear was important for bicycle riders. But he did not know his helmet would help Augie survive a tornado.

Augie lived in Joplin with his mother, Natalie Gonzalez. On May 22, 2011 Gonzalez picked up Augie from baseball practice. Shortly after they returned home, they heard the blare of tornado sirens. Gonzalez looked outside and saw a dark cloud. She made a split-second decision about what to do. She grabbed a blanket and pillow and threw them over her son. Gonzalez also grabbed

◄ **Augie (front) appears on a television show after the storm with Gonzalez (left) and Gonzalez's fiancé (center).**

Augie's bicycle helmet. She had heard that helmets could protect people during natural disasters.

Augie put on his helmet. Then, he and his mother took shelter in the bathtub. The violent winds tore the roof off their home. The pillows kept them warm and helped **insulate** them from the storm. The heavy sides of the tub helped protect them from flying objects. Gonzalez helped shield her son. Suddenly, the toilet in the bathroom ripped from the floor. It flew through the air and struck Augie in the head. But the heavy blow did not hurt him. The helmet kept him safe. It saved his life.

The storm destroyed the family's home, but they were happy to be safe. In August 2011, Augie went back to school. Volunteers donated a backpack with supplies for his first day. Both Augie and his mother saw kids and teachers they had not seen since the storm. "It's nice to see everyone walking through the halls smiling," Gonzalez said.[8]

A few months later, Theilen returned to Kelsey Norman Elementary School. He had heard about Augie's survival story on the news. Theilen brought Augie a special gift: a brand-new bicycle helmet.

STAYING SAFE DURING A TORNADO

People who find shelter are more likely to survive tornadoes. During a tornado, people should stay away from windows and doors. Basements, bathtubs, or hallways with no windows can help protect people from flying objects.

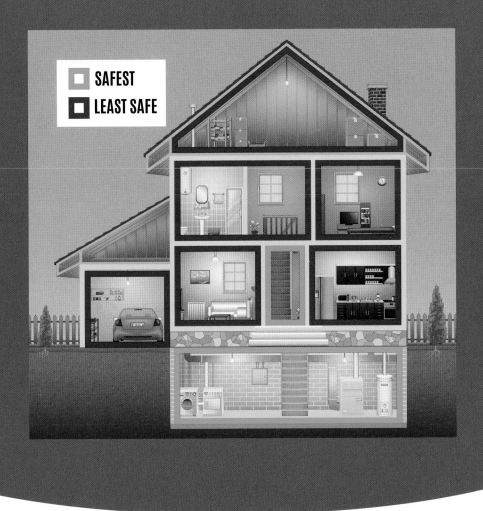

SAFEST

LEAST SAFE

Chapter 4

AN INSPIRING RECOVERY

Seventeen-year-old Quinton Anderson loved football and science. He played for the Joplin High School football team as a backup receiver. Quinton was a straight-A student and dreamed of studying biology in college.

May 22, 2011 was a Sunday. Quinton was at home with his parents when the tornado sirens sounded. His sister, Grace, and a friend were driving back to Joplin from nearby Anderson, Missouri. At 5:30 p.m., Grace stopped to send Quinton a text message about the weather. She asked if she should return home. Quinton noticed the sky was growing darker. He told her to stay where she was in case the weather turned bad.

By about 5:45 p.m., the storm was roaring toward Quinton's neighborhood. It was so big he could not see anything beyond it. He crouched down with his parents in a hallway for protection.

◄ **The Joplin football team makes its way to the field on September 10, 2011.**

Soon, the storm hit, **strewing** debris through every room. The tornado tore the roof off the house. Quinton looked up at the sky. Then, he felt something hit his back. That was the last thing he remembered.

The tornado destroyed the Andersons' home. Quinton was thrown by the tornado. He had several broken bones and bad cuts. Rescue workers found him across the street from his home, near a neighbor's yard. The rescuers took Quinton to the hospital. For three days, he lay unconscious. No one at the hospital could identify him. Quinton's family and friends believed he had died in the storm. When Quinton finally regained consciousness, he told a nurse his name. Soon, he reconnected with Grace and learned that neither of his parents had survived the storm.

For the next five weeks, Quinton stayed in the hospital. His recovery was difficult, and he missed his parents. But he was determined to return to his classes. He chose a motto to help him achieve goals: "Always take that extra step."[9] Grace visited Quinton as he recovered. When he left the hospital, Quinton and Grace moved in with relatives in a nearby town.

The storm had destroyed not only Quinton's home but also his school. The tornado had swept through the building, breaking windows and scattering furniture. When Quinton's principal, Kerry

Sachetta, saw the damage, he said it looked like a bomb had hit the building.

Despite the damage to the building, high school classes resumed as scheduled just 87 days after the tornado. Classes for

▲ **Wreckage sits outside a Joplin school after the 2011 tornado. Half of the schools in the district were damaged or destroyed by the storm.**

the juniors and seniors took place in an abandoned department store because of the damage to the school. Quinton was still recovering from injuries to his legs. But he was determined to get back to school on time, no matter where his classes took place. On August 17, 2011, he walked through the doors of the makeshift school.

Though the high school was gone, the football field remained. Because of his injuries, Quinton could no longer play. But he attended the team's practices and games. His teammates recognized his spirit and leadership. They voted to make him a team captain. The team became a symbol of hope for the town. Thousands showed up to watch the home opener on September 10, 2011.

Quinton also worked hard to participate in other school activities. He played the viola in the school orchestra and began applying to colleges. "There's only one way to go in life, and that's forward," he said.[10]

In 2012, Quinton graduated from Joplin High School. President Barack Obama gave a speech at the ceremony. He praised Quinton's determination to succeed. "In a lot of ways, Quinton's journey has been Joplin's journey," President Obama

Quinton Anderson applauds president Barack Obama, who ▶ spoke at Joplin High School's graduation ceremony on May 21, 2012.

▲ Joplin High School was damaged beyond repair from the tornado. The new high school opened on September 2, 2014.

said.[11] Both Quinton and the city of Joplin had faced difficult challenges. Both had worked hard to recover after the storm. Months after graduating, Quinton achieved one of his goals. He started college at Harding University, studying biology.

JOPLIN HIGH SCHOOL BEFORE AND AFTER THE TORNADO

May 22, 2011: The high school holds its 2011 graduation ceremony. Hours later, the tornado hits the school, destroying the building.

August 17, 2011: A new school year begins. Juniors and seniors attend classes at an empty department store. Freshman and sophomore classes are held in an education center.

September 10, 2011: Thousands of Joplin residents come out to watch Joplin High School's football team play its home opener. An extra 2,000 seats are brought in for the game.

May 21, 2012: President Obama speaks at the 2012 graduation ceremony.

May 22, 2012: Construction begins on a new high school in Joplin.

September 2, 2014: The new Joplin High School building opens.

GLOSSARY

debris (duh-BREE): Debris contains pieces of wreckage or broken things. Tornadoes often scatter debris.

displaced (diss-PLAYST): People are displaced when they need to leave their homes. The tornado displaced many residents of Joplin.

generators (jen-ur-AY-turz): Generators are machines that produce electricity. Backup generators often produce electricity when the power is out.

insulate (in-SUH-layt): People insulate areas to protect them from the weather. Some Joplin residents used cushions or pillows to insulate shelters.

paramedic (pa-ruh-MEH-dik): A paramedic is a person trained to care for others in emergencies. Many people needed to see a paramedic after the tornado.

refuge (REH-fyooj): A refuge is a shelter or place people go to stay safe. During the Joplin tornado, people looked for a refuge from the powerful winds.

strewing (STROO-ing): Strewing means spreading or scattering. When the tornado started strewing wreckage, people took shelter.

Tornado Alley (tor-NAY-doh AL-ee): Tornado Alley is a region of the United States where tornadoes often happen. Joplin, Missouri, is in Tornado Alley.

SOURCE NOTES

1. "A Twister's Fury: In the Path of Destruction." *CNN*. Turner Broadcasting System, Inc., 28 May 2011. Web. 27 Jun. 2015.

2. Eric Adler and Laura Bauer. "Condition Gray: Inside the Hospital as the Joplin Tornado Hit." *KansasCity.com*. Kansas City Star, 18 Jun. 2011. Web. 27 Mar. 2015.

3. "A Twister's Fury: In the Path of Destruction." *CNN*. Turner Broadcasting System, Inc., 28 May 2011. Web. 27 Jun. 2015.

4. "Tornado Survivor Gets the Chance to Thank the Nurse Who Saved Her." *Fox 14 News*. WorldNow, 5 Oct. 2011. Web. 27 Jun. 2015.

5. Ibid.

6. "Joplin Tornado Survivor Glad He Heeded the Sirens for Once." *CNN*. Turner Broadcasting System, Inc., 24 May 2011. Web. 27 Mar. 2015.

7. "IHOP Reopens in Joplin." *Four States Home Page*. Nexstar Broadcasting, Inc., 9 Aug. 2012. Web. 27 Jun. 2015.

8. David Muir and Seni Tienabeso. "Joplin, MO, Students Return to School Three Months after Deadly Tornado." *ABC News*. ABC News Internet Ventures, 17 Aug. 2011. Web. 27 Jun. 2015.

9. Barack Obama. "Remarks by the President at the Joplin High School Commencement." *The White House*. USA.gov, 21 May 2012. Web. 27 Jun. 2015.

10. Ryan Foster. "After Tornado Tragedy, HU Student Looks Ahead, Reflects." *The Bison*. Harding University, 31 Oct. 2012. Web. 27 Jun. 2015

11. Barack Obama. "Remarks by the President at the Joplin High School Commencement." *The White House*. USA.gov, 21 May 2012. Web. 27 Jun. 2015.

TO LEARN MORE

Books

Fradin, Judy, and Dennis Fradin. *Tornado! The Story Behind These Twisting, Turning, Spinning, and Spiraling Storms.* Des Moines, IA: National Geographic Children's Books, 2011.

Gullo, Arthur. *The Power of Nature: Tornadoes.* New York: Cavendish Square Publishing, 2015.

Tarshis, Lauren. *I Survived the Joplin Tornado, 2011.* New York: Scholastic Kids, 2015.

Web Sites

Visit our Web site for links about the Joplin tornado:

childsworld.com/links

Note to Parents, Teachers, and Librarians: We routinely verify our Web links to make sure they are safe and active sites. So encourage your readers to check them out!

INDEX